Never One for Promises

Never One for Promises

Poems by

Sarah A. Etlinger

© 2018 Sarah A. Etlinger. All rights reserved. This material may not be reproduced in any form, published, reprinted, recorded, performed, broadcast, without the express written consent of Sarah A. Etlinger. All such actions are strictly prohibited by law.

Cover design by Shay Culligan

ISBN: 978-1-949229-44-8

Kelsay Books
Aldrich Press
www.kelsaybooks.com

for Valerie—
this would not have been possible without you.

Acknowledgements

"Two Fools," "Geraniums 1", "Geraniums II," "Pears", "Standing in Front of the Montreal Japanese Gardens," and "AshWednesday" appear in Volume 4, Issue 2 of *The Magnolia Review.*

"Chili Pepper" appears in *Lust (Pure Slush)* in April 2018.

"The Collection" appears in the February 2018 issue of *hence, tirade!*

"Before the Flood" appears in *The Gyroscope Review* 18.2 (Winter 2018).

"An Act of God" appears in *Cliterature* 47 (Spring 2018).

"Summer Aubade" will appear as a "Post Poem" in August 2018 from *Raw Dog Review.*

"A Prayer to the God Palace" will appear in the *Unbelief* anthology in August 2018.

Contents

Two Fools	11
The Collection	12
Before the Flood; Or, What Noah's Wife Knew	13
Pangaea	15
Still Life with Poetry	18
Pears	20
Chili Pepper	22
Geraniums (I)	23
Geraniums (II)	24
Standing in Front of the Montreal Japanese Gardens	25
January Thaw	26
An Act of God	28
Unpacking the Last Box After Moving in Together	29
If There Is No Minotaur, the Monster in the Labyrinth Is You	32
Dayenu (It Would Have Been Enough)	33
Summer Aubade	35
Zeus Contemplates his Encounter with Leda While Awaiting His Rape Trial	36
Moment Before the Storm	37
Pillow Talk 2	38
Venus in the Shower	40
A Prayer to the God Palace	41
Ash Wednesday	43

Two Fools

Two fools, we:
sun-baptized and swallowed up.
When we kissed later
in the sizzling rain,
I could taste
the day in your throat.

I wanted to run down the hill,
arms spread out for you.
You wanted to climb up
to the roof at night—
so we could see
the stars, you said.
You said my hair
smelled like patchouli.
I wanted to believe you,
wanted to believe in God
and all that up there,
spread out for us.

We leaned against your car
as you taught me to smoke,
the chest nervous as the breath
jerks in: "Like this—
Hurry up, Mom's coming!"
you said.

I noticed a single stem of cotton
against the rear windshield
tucked like a flower behind the ear.
You were not a Southern boy;
it was a souvenir of a traveler.

The Collection

The red flask of your aftershave
waits on the edge of my sink
while I look for stray hairs.

Do you keep a collection of these
that you leave by the sinks
of women you want
to love you?

Do you keep them
lined up in a closet
next to the towels and toilet paper
and lightbulbs, expecting
transfer to brightly-lit bathrooms
where women scrutinize
each pore, yank each stray hair, in case
you might want to love them today?

When there's a museum
of your love life and they turn it all
into an exhibit,
(including the collection of love notes
from your lovers)
what will the curator say?

Before the Flood; Or, What Noah's Wife Knew

Our therapist said we had to find
the root of the infidelity.
I think I found it, in Noah (and his wife);
he built the boat for twos, not threes:
two this, two that, and it wasn't even raining.

Naamah must have known
how ridiculous it all was, being in a threesome.

She must have seen how his hands
crafted the bow in perfect woman-curves;
curves I see everywhere
in soft ducks' breasts,
in long ears dangling,
in the regular stripes of tigers,
in the lull of the hills
across the horizon.

She must have seen how, as he smoothed
the gopher-wood and pitch
with his soft, worn hands
he was wistful.
Did she see in his eyes
how he loved the way it felt on his skin?

Did his wife see it
the same way I saw it
in your eyes and felt it on your breath
when you came home too late,
came to bed to lie with me
but with the imprint of her curves
on your body?

Naamah must have known—
how ridiculous it all was.

Yes, his wife must have seen it all—
within all those cubits and precise instructions—
when he summoned her to bed
with a promise on his lips
that they would save the world from flooding
to keep everything alive
(*every creeping thing of the earth*
after its kind, two of every kind
will come to you to keep them alive).
Did Naamah ask the same question
I ask you now:
Did god tell you
how to craft the bow
just right, so it would look like
the curve of her hips—
youthful parentheses given life
by your kisses?
(the very same hips
whose soothing curves
ruined this whole complicated business
of pairing?)

Yes, she must have known
how ridiculous it all was
as she stepped onto the ark.

Pangaea

Once the earth was a giant
jagged continent
and you could leap
from India to Africa;
kiss in South America and skip
over to Asia after dinner.
If it rained at your picnic,
you could jump
on over past the equator to bake
in the sun.

In school we pinned flags
in places we'd visited—
noted the passes
through the mountains
and mapped the shortest routes
to the best swimming hole
or where in Lake Victoria
you could get the best fish.
We learned all this
until cracks appeared—

—and then India decided
it didn't want so much
foot traffic, and Madagascar
had a disagreement with Africa
so they split and share
custody of the Mozambique channel,
and slowly
there were countries and continents,
jagged edges in new places
and you couldn't walk
across them anymore

(so they invented planes and ships and trains
but it wasn't the same and now you had to plan your trip).

Once we were waking up
to the curtain
of the morning
spread across our bed;
you had sleep in your hair
and I wore my blue nightgown.

Once you said
"You are the only
one who can save
me." And you kept me,
holy and tender against
your chest like a rosary.

Once you said,
"I don't think any woman
has ever loved a man this way"
— once you were right.

And once I kissed your forehead
like a priest—
and I said,
"Let's take a trip somewhere
warm" so we went.

Once lions roared in China
and you could find tigers
in Africa—

and your bed
seemed like the whole world
mapped out
small and close.

Still Life with Poetry

In the corner of the library,
a couple sits in uncomfortable chairs
with their backs against the sunlight,
elbow-close but not quite touching.
The woman studies an anthology of poetry
thick as a cement block; her delicate
pencil-like fingers turn pages
thinner than fresh butterfly wings
that swat the moisture off in invisible arcs.
She writes a careful note in the margins.

His head is bent over a slim volume
of Kant. His elbow
folded carefully across his chest
the way she folds his shirts
warm out of the dryer.
He never moves, except
when she nudges him with a soft fingertip;
even then, he only slowly unfolds—
(as if emerging from a chrysalis, one limb at a time)
deliberate, smooth movements.
He silently follows her finger
and nods imperceptibly,
and she flips another page.

She turns her head to him, but he is not looking
at her. His eyes stare ahead, flit to his page
and back again. He is bored, there, with her;
I can tell. He is restless; his stare betrays
wanderlust, longing for fulfillment beyond
the pages of philosophers.
Does she know? Can she tell
how he can't hide his boredom?

As she looks back at her book I think
she does know. Her head tilts slightly,
her lips part silently as she makes another circle
on the page.
I wonder what she'll say to him
when they're alone in their grad school apartment,
after the sun has gone down and they sip tea.

Will she finally tell him what she's reading?
Will he tell her, as she curls in the hook of his arm
what he loves about Kant? Will he tell her
how he longs to meet the horizon
at the ocean, how he needs the sting
of spices from a foreign market on his tongue
as he slips in and out, weaving and bobbing
like a displaced local?

Her eyes will burn
from tears as he tells her
it's over, it was over before it started,
("We were out of our element.
You know that. It was never going to work.")

I want to say to her:
"Keep reading Yeats and Rilke and the sonnets.
Keep their heartbreak on your sleeve
for, when you realize he is not for you,
when you realize that love is enough,
but only on these pages,
you'll want your notes."

Pears

I said I'd cut a pear for lunch.
In my hands it looked bulky, squeezed
(as if there were too much inside),
the skin bulbous and stretched,
scars speckled like smeared mascara
over its lumps.

The knife slid too easily through its body.
A perfect slice fell onto the plate suddenly,
as if warning me that a cut is always final.

Later we spread out in the moonlight.
We held each other, the gift of soft touch
on soft bodies whispering each other to sleep.
I traced the eyebrow contours of your face;
my tender lips forgave all those past sins,
erased the stains left by women
who didn't love you enough.
In your sigh—
one pitch lower than post-coital—
I heard mending.

Today, I wonder if it lasted.

Since then, we have learned to love
other people, as one does when one has to.
I had not thought about you
with anything other than my body
and the invisible throb of my heart
in so long, and I can't even remember
why you came over in the first place,
though I suspect it was because we both knew
the pain the skin conceals.

Yesterday, I cut another pear
for my lunch. The light from the window
highlighted a single brown scar
on its skin, and I remembered
that—just before you left me—
I had placed my hands on the hollow
of your chest, as if to anoint
your wounds. As I pressed
on the pear's skin it gave way to reveal
white mealy nectar, concealing
the smooth brown seeds
that I knew were tucked tight in against the core,
protected from tears and scars and harsh
gashes from hungry teeth of women.

Chili Pepper

There's a chili pepper left over
from the salsa my husband made.
I move it to the windowsill
and in my fingers
it seems so light.
Its body curls
like my favorite whorl of your hair;
(his is so straight—like our son's, too)
it curves lazily
like your twisted legs in my bed.

The pepper shares the same red
as my son's fire truck,
the one you stepped on
when you last came over.
Your face puckered
(like you'd eaten the pepper raw);
the pain oily, sharp
on your feet as they skipped
across the floor when you rushed,
naked, throwing your socks behind you,
before you slipped between the sheets to me.

I laughed, then—but later
when I found
a stray sock under the bed,
I realized how much it must have hurt.

Geraniums (I)

I've kept a pot of white geraniums
on the windowsill for a decade.
Each season I trim them back ruthlessly—
right down to the nubs
so they look like the arms of a snowman.
Each season I wonder, "Will this be the last time?
Will this be the time I finally kill them,
cut too deeply or too far down?"

(Once my mother cut them back so far down
I thought she had killed them for sure:
there was nothing but a single stem
sticking up out of the soil in the pot,
a lonely tree with no branches to keep it company
or arms to hug the sunlight.
I thought for sure it would shrivel and die,
and every day I checked it, looking for signs of life.)

One day, I saw a shoot. And then another.
A little green arm reached up out of the soil
and waved, its leaf
 a fuzzy green hand, chubby as a baby's.
After that, so many shoots grew,
I had to separate them into different pots.

Since then I am merciless when I cut them back:
no cut seems too deep or too long.

Geraniums (II)

I love the contrast of white
set against rich green leaves
spread out like fans,
the petals in smiling clusters
growing in ready-made bouquets
proudly bursting from the stems.

The leaves are soft, soft
like the inside of your thigh
when I brush it with my lips, when my hand
caresses it all the way down to your ankles.

Sometimes I think I want to plant your feet
in the soil, and water you
so you soak up
nutrients.

Or maybe I could grow
another one of you.
Maybe you would sprout
a seedling, a leaf—
maybe I'd finally cut you back enough
(down to your roots)
so you would have no choice
but to bloom.

As you lie there with me
and I fall asleep, a tendril
curled against your arm,
I dream of a whole row
of rich, terra-cotta flowerpots
holding seedlings lovingly
snipped from your feet.

Standing in Front of the Montreal Japanese Gardens

There you are, an oily smudge
in the center of a photo taken by a passing tourist:
you're squinting because the sun faces you,
but you're smiling, and your thin squared arm
curls around my waist. I'm smiling, too,
behind big sunglasses. Thin from Paris
I am wearing jeans too young for me
and you look like you just rolled out of bed
in a too-big T-shirt, bagging jeans
that I cinched at your smooth, quadrangular waist
after I blew you, standing in front of the window.
You'd leaned backwards over the radiator,
your face like you'd seen Jesus, finally;
his twisted body dangling from the golden cross
stuck to your neck.

In the photo, behind us, a full skirt of sun drapes
across the red pagoda, and carp swim carelessly,
smoothly in the algae-darkened pond.
They don't know where they are;
they just keep gliding, silken and peaceful.

They don't know that later,
when it's dark and the only light
comes from the cigarette bobbing
between your tight lips as you walk
through the city, I am pretending to sleep.

January Thaw

Outside the window
rumors of spring's quickness
fall on the breath of trees, branches
stretch their arms after long naps.

Birds chitter in coffee klatches
perched atop wires and huddled
in patchwork nests cajoled

from pieces of lint and fuzz,
spare twigs and scraps
of plastic bags for lashings.

Brimful clouds hold up the sky,
pinned carefully along the precise
cut of horizon—
white and gray and handfuls of blue.

The clear mirth of a full brook
giggles over rocks,
carving and flexing

like your peckish finger
over my spine and rounding
the bends of my hips.

Inside, I can hear
your sleeping breath,
the metronome
by which our time is measured.

The brief gasp of January's thaw
reminds me of spring—
when I grew to love you.

Tomorrow, ice will coat
the windowpanes, easy
as your breath on my neck,
and just as cold.

An Act of God

I saw God on the subway today.
At first, I didn't recognize him
because he wore a gray suit
with a crisp shirt and tie.
But then I saw
the label on his briefcase
and the black licorice smile of his eyes.

He saw me
and put his hands
on my breast
to inspect what he had created
and he saw that it was good.

Unpacking the Last Box After Moving in Together

I found the last photo you have of her:
she is standing in front of the black, slick rocks
and graying waves that reach to the shore.
Her dark glossy hair glistens in the sun.
Glasses off, she smiles, half-squints:
she wants you to see her eyes
but you know she is nearly blinded
by sun; by sand-riddled air; by wind gusts gentle
and fierce at the same time.
An arabesque of hair freezes
above her head; her feet shade the sand
in a lithe, languorous line.

I see her dress but I am not looking at it.
I know she carries a straw bag
for the beach (and your kids' stuff)
and I know her toes smile out of her shoes.

I know that she has beads of ocean water on her arms;
that sand has painted up her legs; that just before this
you watched her swim, your eyes following
as the waves hiccupped around her speckled
eggshell skin.

I know that just before this— she glides out of the water—
just before this—and just after she drank a beer—her lips
grazing the top of the bottle—you said,
"Smile!" and, like a seagull snatching the last morsel
of a beach picnic, you caught her
before she could smile.

I know all this, but I do not see it. Instead
I am looking at the squints of her eyes, trying to find a clue
that would explain everything:
Why she left the kids alone to almost drown
so she could drink a beer.
Why she hopped into bed after bed after bed all those nights.
What she was looking for.

For you I search closely, carefully, squinting my eyes to match hers.
Maybe I can see through hers this way.
I am looking at her bare fingernails, her freckled neck;
her shoulders half-hidden by the wide straps of her sundress.
Her body is so different from mine—this brown goddess,
this brunette Venus.
I am looking at her—
looking at her looking at you
on the beach, the sun loving her
only half as much as you do.
I am looking at her and I know—
just from looking—
that she will break your heart,
for there you are, your big toe
snuck into the frame just off center.

It is not, now, Ogunquit, Maine, in August.
(It is February in Wisconsin and it is frigid.)
My own body is pink, rosy, messy—I am not smiling
or squinting in summer beach light.
My tea-stained eyes are open in a moving stare.
I have rings of pale fat around my neck

*(you say you love
this plump necklace; you nuzzle me there
when we make love and you sigh when it's over,
content. I do not believe
you are completely happy).*

I have ragged toenails covered
with gray argyle socks.
But as I stare at her,
in this last photo,
I am no longer so envious,
for she mocks the sunlight
even though it loves her so.

You catch me looking at this (not too old) photo
and I think you know—in the split second
your eyes search mine—
I am sure we know—
that there will never be another day like that;
that what is once lost may never be found—
yet, as your fingers reach to my neck, this place you love,
I know, too, that one day someone might look at you
looking at me this way.

Someone will see you, leaning against the bathroom
counter, mirror behind your head,
solemn, almost in prayer
(do you pray to me the way you loved her?)
but they will not find a shadow in a squint;
they will not see your bruised heart as it beats
crooked beats hidden under the fold of your robe.

That is mine to tend, I think, with ardor.

If There Is No Minotaur, the Monster in the Labyrinth Is You

I. Ariadne's Thread

We stood in front of that tree,
      noses close, as if
your little finger pulled a thread
and charmed our faces together.
Each moment springloaded, staring
      into your eyes, against the rain
painting a stain on your shirt
      I could never wash out
of my memory.

II. Bull in a China Shop

I never did kiss you—
      I just clung to your heartbeat
like the fraying end of a thread
      or a dying leaf at the end of a branch
twisting and pulling in different directions
      in the wind and the rain
all I did
      was let you loose
along the restless angles
      of the city—the stars
no guide for your manic
      zigzag; the night
no solace for your lonely wanderlust.

Dayenu (It Would Have Been Enough)

I.

Once there was nothing but the ways of goddesses
and ambrosial kisses christening sleep.

In the morning, the demons come out in layers,
trochaic echoes recalling blinked heartbeats.

Now, in the voice through the fog
creep uneven reverberations.

The whiff of regret wafts through the cracks
in the blinds, displacing light.

II.

In your memory the body is a halted tumble after laughter
and even in the mirth of new roses and Riesling

the fervent, hulking tremolos—
    dayenu (enough), *dayenu* (enough), *dayenu* (enough)

rise like the tide in your throat,
the missed promise from a blighted eucharist.

III.

Martyred passion —denial's mournful sainthood—
writes too deeply on your body

for salvation, even when she says
I love you

from warbles deep in her throat
that sound like rain.

Summer Aubade

Sometimes we feel more than we ever are:

hammocked in your arms
we fade into summer's
constellations
displayed for us
only us

until dawn erases the stars.

Zeus Contemplates his Encounter with Leda While Awaiting His Rape Trial

(Later, he would say)

She looked like a holiday,
bare in embrace;
girlish and slick,
she giggled until it was over.
Smudged smiles etched
into the skin,
carrying the scent
of bodies loved in full sun.

(Back in the clouds,
he remembered)

she hallowed his back
with her breath; she
unfolded each wing—
delicate as white brocade,
smooth as the sun
on the water—
with careful fingers
and pregnant pink lips
caressing each feather,
each weary sinew
in holy consecration.

(After it was all over
and he flew back to his celestial palace
he would remember)

that they slept, holy and restful
amidst a cathedral of blankets
two halves of a broken whole.

Moment Before the Storm

Your eyes hold the light
of our memories
that glisten in the back of my throat.

Pillow deep and soft,
I whisper (between the arcs
of stars and space),
we are but breath
mere vapors and traces,

as we unfold,
lost in the dust of dreams.

Pillow Talk 2

He said
he wanted to keep me company
in my insomnia, so
we sat, knees mountains
in the bed,
hands held across
the valleys they made,
our bodies ink
on the pillows and creases.
I think it would be interesting
if you wrote a poem
about life before
women got their periods

I said
nothing
because that has never
happened and what
would life be like without it?
(This is what he says
when he thinks he is funny.)
But then I think of Venus
arising from a shell
bobbing among the waves,
Adriatic green:
she had babies,
she had a womb
blood-red and holy
enough for twins.

He said
I worry about you
so much, awake at night
and he strokes my head,
his fingers tendrils
across my face.

I cannot help but think
he writes me into existence
like the fashioning of angels,
(pale waxen skin
new against the silhouette
of morning)
a Venus without her period—
barren, virginal, fresh and clean
as the night air
he breathes into his sleeping lungs.

Venus in the Shower

Angry marbles of water
are no match for the pearline
etiquette of her skin;
rose or white or deep blue
it still commands
the worship
of every man who sees her.

Suds cling in lacy patches
like a wedding dress
before they disappear,
catching the kinky tresses
that circle the drain.

Oily from shampoo grease,
she wishes for once
the razor might cut
and draw blood.

A Prayer to the God Palace

I prayed to a god I don't even believe in;
I prayed to him or her or it, or them—
(God and Jesus and Mary and Joseph
and Yahweh and Allah and Sheba
and Amon-Ra –Amon Ra twice because I like his name—
and Ceres and Persephone, and Isis
and Hera and Zeus, king and queen of the sky
and the Pope)
I prayed to *all of them*
asking them "Please please *please*"
because I know you wouldn't ever ask
if you didn't need salvation;
if you didn't need my crooked broken
rosary song in a choking garbled mantra
(Amen Amen Amen holy
Amen Amen).

I prayed to *all of them*
and when they heard my voice
they turned to each other and looked
(because they all live up there in the sky
together, in a golden god-palace;
some peering out windows and some sitting on god-thrones
and some waiting with holy children on the couches)
"Who is that?" –a new voice they don't know
among the chanting cacophony.

I prayed to *all of them*
for your peace of mind;
for the sweet release of sleep.
I speak with upturned face:
"Please, please please"
hoping in my pleas they can also read my mind
(Amen Amen Amen holy

Amen Amen)
hoping they know
how to give you a shadow of sleep
in moonlight's soft comma
and how I could kiss your tears;
(My grandmother used to say
we were part Eskimo because we both loved
the cold, cold ocean.
I would hope the waves broke on my ankles
and legs so I could taste the salt on my lips,
on my tongue, at the back of my throat);
I know now this was so I would learn
to love tears' bitter salt baptism.

I pray to *all of them* (Amen amen amen holy
amen amen)
up there in their god-palace
hoping they can see
how I dream of you; how I can feel
the way your body wrote on mine
holy watermarks, prayer scars
and tattooed bands of tefillin
weaving through my fingers, crossing
my palms and wrists,
a benevolent crucifixion, really—
your blood my blood god's blood
holy water in my veins.

Ash Wednesday

Spring unfurls, slowly,
greeted by ashes on the forehead
like kisses from burnt ghosts.

You were never one for promises—
the only promise you kept
a smear of ashes
from Ash Wednesday;
a proud burn
of salt and carbon
above your eyebrows.

These ashes remind me
of your hand, spectral
outlines in the dark
as mine rested upon it
while we drove, cosmic travelers
in the night,
ashes from your cigarette
falling among the stars.

No, you would never promise anything,
(not even in spring):
you would always only remember
that you were once dust, and that you'd return.

Notes

Like a garden, a book cannot grow without attention, nourishment, a stroke of luck, and favorable conditions. The following people have provided the optimal conditions for growing this book so that it could thrive.

First, there would be no book or even garden plot without Kathleen Dale, who serves as my patient, tolerant, mentor/coach. She has seen the potential of each word and nourished each seedling so that it could bloom gloriously. Without her expert reading, questions, and guidance—-as well as the bottomless coffee—none of this would have happened. Thank you, Kathleen! Other important sources of nourishment come from other writers and readers such as Molly Sides; Becky Hansen (whose submission challenge started it all); Liana Odrcic; Colleen Halverson; and Kevin Wozniak (who, for nearly 20 years, has believed in me and my craft, even when it was hiding). Thank you. Thanks also to Carol Ostrom, Derrick Harriell, Allison Castillo, Joann Heck-Meiter, Beth Ingle, Stuart Moulthrop, and Martin Quirk for all of your support and love.

Thank you to the two best readers a poet could have: Pam Inglese and Lisa Kortebein. Your guidance and support has been indispensable; thank you both so much for being my champions and my sounding board. To my reviewers, Dr. Elizabeth Johnston and Suzannah Anderson—thank you for seeing my book in ways I did not.

For my wonderful family: Brad Houston (the most incredible, loving, supportive, and steadfast husband a woman could want—thank you, thank you, thank you, for loving me and cheering me on. I am lucky to have you on my team and you will always have all my love); my son Gabriel whose infectious smile and zest for life has inspired me and forced me to be brave; my parents (Ron and Kathy Etlinger) for always believing in me; my sister Audrey Cohen for cheering me on, buying my poems/book and for ensuring I would get paid. Thank you! My aunt Patty Lavoie and cousin Mary will always be my role models and champions—thank you for your unconditional love.

Finally, to two people who have become my family, and whom I could not live without: Paul Laprade, what can I say? From the first moment we became friends, I have been in awe of you and your ability to see things in people; you saw in me something I did not, and drew it out in a way no one else could have. In essence, this project is yours as much as it is mine—thank you for calling into being my poetry. Thank you for your friendship, your readership, your love of W.S. Merwin and of poetry, and for your presence in the world—it means more to me than I can write.

and to Valerie Blair—I have dedicated this to you because your love and guidance and friendship illuminates every page. I could not, would not have done this without you. Thank you so very much for being my roadie, my sounding board, my ad-hoc nanny, my fellow foodie, my reality check, my sister patriarchy-smasher, and everything in between. For you, the first book, because it represents so many firsts and implies, of course, that there will be more. I hope we can have more of everything! Thank you.

About the Author

Sarah A. Etlinger holds a Ph.D. in English and works as an English professor. She resides in Milwaukee, WI, with her family (a husband, young son, and cocker spaniel mix). Though she hails from New England, Milwaukee is her adopted home. Her work can be found in many journals and magazines including *The Penwood Review, Cliterature,* and *Little Rose Magazine;* and she can be found discussing her work in The Poetry Professors' podcast (episode 107). Interests other than poetry include cooking, traveling, reading, and learning to play piano.

www.ingramcontent.com/pod-product-compliance
Lightning Source LLC
LaVergne TN
LVHW091321080426
835510LV00007B/591